Maya Angelou,

Her Phenomenal
Life & Poetic Journey

From the Editors of
ESSENCE

ESSENCE

EDITOR-IN-CHIEF Vanessa K. Bush
DEPUTY MANAGING EDITOR Dawnie Walton
CREATIVE DIRECTOR Erika N. Perry
EDITORIAL PROJECTS DIRECTOR
Patrik Henry Bass
EDITORIAL OPERATIONS DIRECTOR
Denolyn Carroll

FROM THE EDITORS OF ESSENCE
MAYA ANGELOU
HER PHENOMENAL LIFE & POETIC JOURNEY

EDITOR Patrik Henry Bass
DESIGN DIRECTOR Sandra Lawrence
PHOTO DIRECTOR Adreinne Waheed
PRODUCTION MANAGER Raphael Joa
REPORTERS Bridgette Bartlett-Royall,
Ylonda Gault Caviness
COPY EDITORS Valerie A. David, Janice K. Bryant

CONTENT CREDITS
ESSENCE acknowledges all the writers
who contributed to this book:
Dr. Maya Angelou, asha bandele,
Tonya Bolden, Pearl Cleage, Edwidge Danticat,
Rita Dove, Nikky Finney,
Melissa Harris-Perry, Sonia Sanchez

SPECIAL THANKS
Michelle Ebanks, Maria Beckett, Carina A. Rosario,
Andrea Jackson, Amy Glickman, Akkida McDowell,
Monique Manso, Armando Correa, Dawn Abbott,
Mary F. Yearwood of the Schomburg Center for
Research in Black Culture

PUBLISHER Jim Childs
VICE PRESIDENT AND ASSOCIATE PUBLISHER
Margot Schupf
VICE PRESIDENT, FINANCE Vandana Patel
EXECUTIVE DIRECTOR, BUSINESS DEVELOPMENT
Suzanne Albert
EXECUTIVE DIRECTOR, MARKETING SERVICES
Carol Pittard
EXECUTIVE DIRECTOR, MARKETING
Susan Hettleman
PUBLISHING DIRECTOR Megan Pearlman
ASSOCIATE DIRECTOR OF PUBLICITY
Courtney Greenhalgh
ASSISTANT GENERAL COUNSEL Simone Procas
ASSISTANT DIRECTOR, SPECIAL SALES
Ilene Schreider
SENIOR MARKETING MANAGER, SALES MARKETING
Danielle Costa
MARKETING MANAGER Isata Yansaneh
ASSOCIATE PRODUCTION MANAGER
Kimberly Marshall
ASSOCIATE PREPRESS MANAGER
Alex Voznesenskiy
ASSOCIATE PROJECT MANAGER Amy Mangus
- -
EDITORIAL DIRECTOR Stephen Koepp
SENIOR EDITOR Roe D'Angelo
COPY CHIEF Rina Bander
DESIGN MANAGER Anne-Michelle Gallero
EDITORIAL OPERATIONS Gina Scauzillo

SPECIAL THANKS

Katherine Barnet, Brad Beatson, Jeremy Biloon,
Susan Chodakiewicz, Rose Cirrincione,
Assu Etsubneh, Mariana Evans, Christine Font,
David Kahn, Jean Kennedy, Courtney Mifsud,
Nina Mistry, Dave Rozzelle, Ricardo Santiago,
Divyam Shrivastava, Holly Smith, Adriana Tierno

Published by ESSENCE Books, an imprint of
Time Home Entertainment Inc.
135 W. 50th St. • New York NY 10020

**We welcome your comments and suggestions
about ESSENCE Books. Please write to us at:**
ESSENCE Books
Attention: Book Editors
P.O. Box 11016
Des Moines IA 50336-1016

If you would like to order any of our hardcover
Collector's Edition books, please call us at
800-327-6388 (Monday through Friday, 7 A.M.–8 P.M.,
or Saturday, 7 A.M.–6 P.M. Central Standard Time).

FRONT COVER Photograph by Patrick Fraser/Corbis
Outline

BACK COVER Photograph by Marlene Wallace

ISBN 10: 1-61893-147-4
ISBN 13: 978-1-61893-147-4
Library of Congress Control Number: 2014942962

contents

Introduction
Vanessa K. Bush 6

Artist
Maya Angelou 14
Edwidge Danticat 30
Pearl Cleage 34

Activist
asha bandele 52
Sonia Sanchez 66
Melissa Harris-Perry 72
Maya Angelou 74

Sisterfriend
Nikky Finney 84
Rita Dove 88

Timeline
Tonya Bolden 96

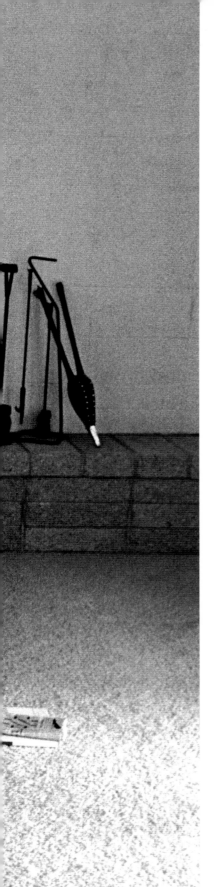

Maya Angelou was, is and always will be a force of nature. There was little Dr. Angelou couldn't do. She was a performer and a peacemaker. Vivacious and visionary. A mother and a muse. She's the first true example of a Black woman I read about who made her own choices about the life she wanted to lead, and refused to allow anyone or anything—not her race, her sex or her economic circumstances—to get in her way. Maya Angelou believed we should live our lives without limits, and in doing so, showed us how we can—how we must—follow this principle.

Just hearing her speak with that deep vibrato made you want to sit up taller and own the space you inhabit with a sense of purpose and pride. Still, it is her transformational storytelling we will most remember. She had a way of being profound without being preachy. Her prose and poetry revealed a deep understanding of our humanity. She wasn't afraid to speak the truth about who we are, or to challenge us to elevate our expectations and life experiences in order to be the best we could be.

Her influence on all of our lives—which resonates from grade-school classrooms to global stages and everywhere in between—has made an indelible imprint on the world that will live on forever.

In our unique celebration of her life and legacy, we've captured her brilliance as an artist, activist and sisterfriend. You'll find close to 100 unforgettable images, some seldom seen, that showcase how dynamic she truly was, as well as loving tributes from icons, peers and admirers. You'll also enjoy homages to Angelou from asha bandele, Pearl Cleage, Edwidge Danticat, Rita Dove, Nikky Finney, Melissa Harris-Perry and Sonia Sanchez. Maya built the platform for modern Black women to have a voice. Here, they raise their eloquent voices to celebrate Angelou's extraordinary legacy. We've also included one of Maya's most compelling essays to ESSENCE within our homage. She was one of our earliest champions and best cheerleaders.

We hope you will enjoy this remembrance of her many contributions. They are evidence of a life well lived. For us, she will always be a phenomenal woman.

Vanessa K. Bush

VANESSA K. BUSH
Editor-in-Chief

A true Renaissance woman—poet, dancer, singer and author—Angelou also appeared in the 1977 classic, *Roots*, based on Alex Haley's best-selling novel.

Artist

"African religions
encourage the
supplicant to
respect the spirit
in the tree,
in the water,
in the flower,
in the air,
in a child.
I, too, am aware
of the presence
of spirit
in everything."

A focused Maya putting words to paper in 1974. Like most great artists, she had a method to how she created and it included having a deck of cards and a crossword puzzle nearby.

10

"I am convinced that most
people do not grow up.
We find parking spaces and
honor our credit cards.
We marry and dare to have children
and call that growing up.
I think what we do is mostly grow old.
We carry accumulation of years
in our bodies and on our faces, but
generally our real selves,
the children inside, are
still innocent and shy as magnolias."

❝Not everything you write is going to be a masterpiece. Not everything you cook is great, not everything you paint—but you're trying for it. From the moment you put the pen to paper or sit down at the piano, you're trying for it.❞

Angelou shares the stage with (left to right) Cicely Tyson, Queen Latifah and Jill Scott.

Angelou (right) performs a concert with Valerie Simpson and Nick Ashford on February 14, 1996, in New York City.

Angelou at the Grammy Awards on March 1, 1994, in New York City. She won an award in the Spoken Word category.

MAYA ANGELOU

In celebration of
our 25th anniversary,
Angelou shared her
passionate perspective
about the triumphant
journey of Black women
in America.

I can't believe my good fortune, and I'm just so grateful, to be a Black woman. A Black American woman. I would be so jealous if I were anything else.

I remember saying this in a small group somewhere, and a white man actually said to me, "Now, come on, you know you wish you were a white man." I laughed so hard, I almost cried. I said, "Absolutely not! I cannot imagine having so much power and yet being incapable of using it in a positive way. I dare not even conjecture what it would do to my psyche, to know that the factors that created my supposedly privileged place in society are the very

have used a number of ploys to erect my own brides over boiling waters, laughing when I wasn't tickled and scratching when I didn't itch. And I'm here—still here, despite the odds.

Being a woman is not about being born female; being born with certain genitalia will only make a person an old whatever-the-genitalia-dictates if the person lives long enough. To be a woman is to take responsibility for your actions and for the time you consume and the space you occupy. It is to strive for constancy in all things—to stretch, to grow, to be courageous enough to change course or change your mind as you discover new truths. It is about assuming the

IN HER OWN WORDS

reasons I am prevented from using whatever power I have for good. It must be an awful burden to bear—to know that if I tried to use my power in a positive way, my people would laugh at me, scorn me, jeer me, and probably disown me. So no, I have no desire to trade places with a white man."

As a Black woman, I know where I have come from. I have nursed a nation of strangers. People I knew would grow up to threaten and maim and kill my own; I have nursed them. I have held together our greatest institutions, the family and the church, and kept the Black man at the top. I have come out of the fields of Alabama, out of the Mississippi Delta, out of the deserts of Texas. I have been creative, constantly taking chances—racehorse chances—to negotiate my path. I

responsibility to find yourself within yourself, to find your own personal power source. To be a woman is to defy outright any idea that would put you in a trick bag, that would inhibit growth, that would bind and limit. To be a woman is to compel yourself to search out and embrace ideas that liberate, that make you bigger, finer, stronger, more courageous, more generous, more merciful. To be a woman is to work hard, to count on yourself, to owe nothing. It is to hold the reins of your life in your own hands.

While there were other groups of women who were pushed to the edge and jumped off or surrendered or gave up, and lots of other folks who have capitulated to blows and slings and arrows of outrageous fortune, Black women have stood up strong every time. I don't know why; I can't explain why this is so. But I know that we have, and I know that we do. Perhaps we are made strong by struggle. It is in this sense that I believe my story is a Black woman's story, and my life the life of a Black woman.

I was raped when I was a girl, and was approached many times after that by people who were interested in me sexually, just sexually. At sixteen I had a baby, and at seventeen I took my baby and hit the road, grabbing any job that came my way so I could keep my baby on my hip. One might have been inclined to think, "Well, this makes me a woman." But really, I was just a female.

My mother was the first person who gave me my first inkling that I was a woman. I was about twenty-one years old and had gone to visit her in San Francisco. I was holding down two jobs at the time, still raising my child by myself, living on my own. Life was always tough—I was always close to the edge, barely hanging on—but I never would ask her for help, even though I knew she gladly would have given it.

You're the greatest woman I've ever met.

We had had lunch and we walked down the hill together, and when we got to the bottom of the hill she turned to me and said very sweetly, "Baby, you know something? I think you're the greatest woman I've ever met." I looked at her, Vivian Baxter, this little five-foot-four woman dressed in a beautiful suit and wearing a wonderful fur and diamond earrings, and she said, "Yes, because you're very intelligent and you're very kind, and those two qualities are rarely found together. So you are a great woman." Then she said, "Give me a kiss." I kissed her, and she crossed the street and got into her yellow Pontiac. I crossed the street the other way and waited for the streetcar.

I got on the streetcar—I remember it so clearly, the time of day, the way the sun hit the seats—and I sat there and thought to myself, "Suppose she's right? Suppose I really am somebody? Suppose I really am a great woman?" I began to look at myself with these two jobs raising a child, being independent and kind, and I thought, "Well, maybe I am!"

It was a glorious, precious moment when this affirmation and self-realization came to me, so many years after my wonderful brother, Bailey—who is almost two years older than I and the closest my family has ever come to producing a genius—had told me that I was very smart. "All knowledge is spendable currency, depending on the market," I remember him saying to me when I was about ten years old, quoting from some book he had read. This one sentence had made such an impression on him that he wanted it to have meaning for me, too. And so, to please him—because I knew he loved me and would never lie to me, telling me I was smart if I really wasn't—I tried to learn everything. By then, Mama, my paternal grandmother, a very powerful woman who had raised me, had brought me to the realization that I was a single person, that I belonged to myself. That, however, did not inform me that I was a woman. It was Vivian Baxter, my mother, who freed me. She fixed me firmly in an understanding of womanhood. She anointed me a woman person.

No one owes this woman, Maya Angelou, anything. No one. And so I marvel at my good fortune and I am very, very grateful. I rejoice that people love me, and that I've reached age sixty-six feeling and looking pretty good, and am still out here doing things that have meaning for me. I believe in hard work, and I see evidence now of the work I've put in. But I know, as a Christian woman and religious person, that I have

Angelou speaks her mind during an interview on June 3, 1974, in Washington, D.C.

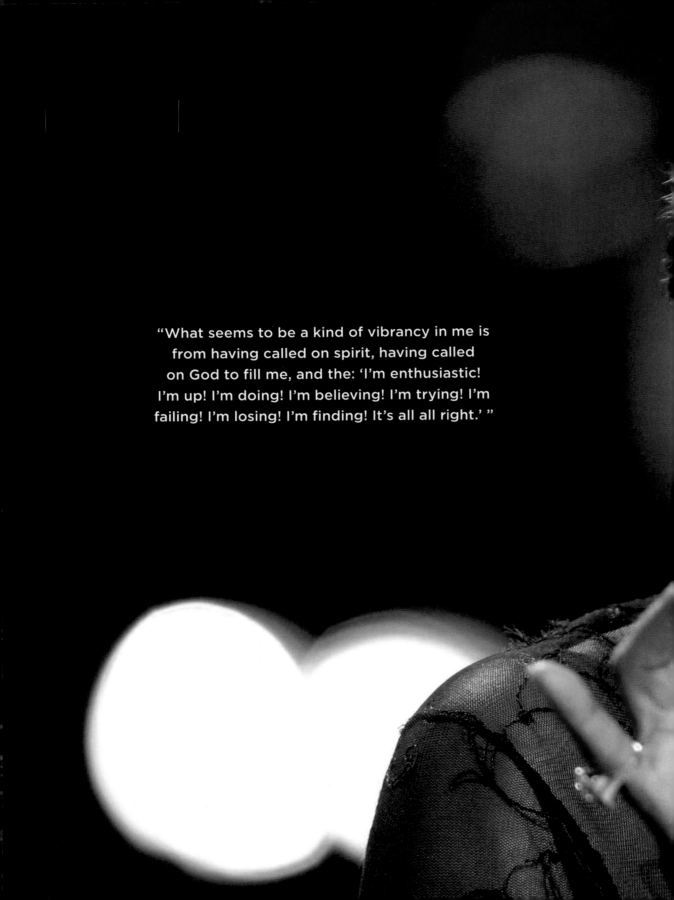

"What seems to be a kind of vibrancy in me is from having called on spirit, having called on God to fill me, and the: 'I'm enthusiastic! I'm up! I'm doing! I'm believing! I'm trying! I'm failing! I'm losing! I'm finding! It's all all right.' "

Angelou delivering a captivating speech at the Democratic National Convention on January 28, 2004, in Boston.

19

been saved and protected from some things that could have ended my life and ended it very badly. In the end, some chances I took served me very well; others did not. But nothing is owed me, and I take nothing for granted—not my life, not my gifts, not my talents, not love.

There is a fabulous Ethiopian song my friends taught me thirty years ago that was banned in Addis Ababa by Emperor Haile Selassie. The song's message is meant to make the listener very uncomfortable and fix a humbling thought in the mind, which is why I like it. It says: "Don't tell me how beautiful you are, or how rich you are, or what a high position you hold, or how pretty you are, or how wise. For if you do, you will make me take you to the edge of the world and show you where people far better off than you have tried to jump off." So I take nothing for granted—including the heady, wonderful privilege of being a Black woman. This is not a passive exercise; it requires work that at times can be very painful. Pain often accompanies privilege.

Built into the privilege of being a Black woman should be an ever-present consciousness that we have been, and still are, targeted for attack. This consciousness should inform our actions, our decisions, and our sense of who we are and what we are about. But we should be careful not to allow it to overwhelm or immobilize us. Rather than allowing my mind to be preoccupied with these negative forces, I direct my energy toward moving on, moving ahead. Instead, I am preoccupied with another program—inquiring about and discovering the world, the environment around me, and how I and my people fit into it and have interacted with it. I am preoccupied observing the truth of Einstein's theory of relativity—that there's no such thing as regression in life, only constant change.

In the past twenty-five years, we have witnessed, as Black women, enormous change, the greatest being an increased awareness and, in many instances, realization of our power. It is, I believe, one of our most significant achievements. In black associations and neighborhood groups, in civic and religious groups, in sororities and political parties, in the corporate world and the public sector, in practically every sphere of influence, Black women are wielding real, actual power, and it is helping in concrete, measurable ways to improve the nature of our existence as a race of people. We can put a company out of business if we decide that it isn't treating our people right. We can make the difference in the outcomes of political elections. Our views help shape the formulation of governmental policies. Our voices are speaking for our people who live under the yoke of tyranny and oppression all over the world.

But though we have gained a lot of power, we have also sustained enormous damage. Nowhere is this more evident than in what is happening to our families. Until about thirty years ago, it seemed we advanced and we pulled our people with us; we pulled our families with us. Like the turtle that carries its babies on its back, it was the way we Black women came through slavery and managed our affairs, somehow, through the hoax of Reconstruction, through the years of lynching, through the years of migrations and perpetual dislocations. Now it appears that the strings that had held us together have been untied

> # I take nothing for granted including the heady privilege of being a Black woman.

Angelou enjoying a
moment of solitude.

and we're seeing the result—the children are running crazy in the streets.

The challenge before us as Black women is to re-establish family ties and to create family, bound by blood or not. This, I am convinced, is our mandate. This is how we save ourselves as a people.

The best place to start, of course, is at home, where all virtues and vices begin. By *home* I don't just mean the physical setting in which we live; I mean that which is harbored within the breast, within the heart of the individual. A tree with a simple root structure won't survive a strong wind, but a tree whose roots go deep into the soil and is firmly anchored stands a far better chance. So it is with us, by anchoring ourselves in a spirituality which we set out in a purposeful, deliberate way to discover. And once we discover it, and we define it, and we cherish it, we are free to spread it and share it with our beloveds, our family and friends, and even people who aren't in our immediate circle. This is when we are at our best.

But even when we are at our worst, at our lowest ebb, we cannot waste time bemoaning our state, and we certainly can't give anybody the delicious satisfaction of knowing they have knocked us down and kept us there. When we are knocked down, we must pick ourselves up as quickly as we can and get on with the business of saving our lives before life dribbles away. Sometimes we can get so low, feel so betrayed, that we begin to question our own worth and think that we don't deserve love. When this happens, we should recognize and acknowledge that we have been wounded, but we should learn also to cauterize our wounds, to sear them shut until we have the luxury of time and the strength of heart to revisit and unseal them for examination. Our spirit and soul can drain through our wounds, if we allow.

Black woman to Black woman, we should be care-ful of anything that threatens to separate us, for if we are separated, we will be undone as a race. This is why I pay no attention whatsoever to the silliness some people would encourage us to dwell upon. What does it matter, for example, if a woman wants to frizz her hair or straighten it, or wear it natural or braid it, cut it all off or wear a wig? We can choose anything we think enhances our beauty. Any idea is at its best when it liberates. Freedom is the right to live the way we want, for, in the end, our lives are all we really have, and only we have the authority to deconstruct and reconstruct ourselves.

Black women for centuries have had to depend on other Black women to keep ourselves, our homes, our institutions and our communities together. With the conditions that loom before us as a people and the awesome challenges we face, it would be genocidal to break the bond of sisterhood. This is why I make a conscious effort to say to my sisterfriends that I love and cherish them, that my life is diminished without their presence and participation in it. I thank them for being in my corner. We try to find wonderful things to say to each other that we really mean—"I love seeing you." "You look great." "You're important to my eyes and ears." We give each other little gifts, or send cards, or call just to say hello. In short, my sisterfriends and I have resolved to hold on to and be there for each other, all the way. I have absolute faith that I could lean on any one of them and she wouldn't buckle; their expectations of me are exactly the same.

Shoring each other up, Black women do that as a rule. My sincerest wish is we hold fast to it, and do it with love. We show that we believe by our own loving actions. Through love we teach. Through love we instruct. Through love we build up.

© 1995 Maya Angelou

> # "We cannot waste time bemoaning our state."

Angelou in 1983 enjoying peace in her Northern California garden.

"You can never be great at anything unless you love it."

(Clockwise, from left) Angelou and Oprah Winfrey in 1993 on the set of the TV movie, *There Are No Children Here;* Diahann Carroll consoles then child actress Constance Good in a scene from the made-for-TV movie, *I Know Why the Caged Bird Sings* in 1979; Angelou on the set of the 1993 film, *Poetic Justice;* Cicely Tyson and Angelou look lovingly at a baby in a scene from the multiple Emmy-winning miniseries, *Roots.*

"Our ability to have and to live on faith brought us through conditions more horrific than we can even imagine. Whenever I get out of touch with my power, I think of our people, in their chains, having no names, not being able to move one inch without the license of someone who purportedly owned them."

Be a rainbow in someone else's cloud.

Head of the class

"My mission in life is not
merely to survive,
but to thrive; and
to do so with
some passion,
some compassion,
some humor,
and some style."

Our Maya

by Edwidge Danticat

The first time I heard Dr. Maya Angelou speak, I was in my early twenties and was a graduate student in the creative writing program at Brown University. She dazzled a packed hall filled with people of all ages and races, and had us laughing, crying, singing, all in one glorious hour. During the question-and-answer session, a woman stood up, and with tears in her eyes, told Dr. Angelou that she had saved her life. She wasn't speaking metaphorically either. She'd been planning her suicide, she said, when she came across one of Dr. Angelou's poems, and after reading it, she vowed to go on living.

Over the years, I would hear the same thing at many of Dr. Angelou's events. Some expressed this out loud and others only muttered it to themselves or to the men and women sitting or standing close by. Dr. Angelou's words had brought them back from the brink of despair. Her bountiful gifts, both on a stage and on the page, had more than inspired; they had saved lives.

This is one of the most powerful gifts any artist can hope to offer the world: a life's work that soars beyond Art, into the realm of survival. We were not mere spectators or consumers of Dr. Angelou's multi-layered, multi-media work. We were fellow travelers on a sometimes brutal and sometimes exuberant journey. We were her kin, her confidantes, guests at her dinner table. We were her sisters, daughters, her sister friends.

This was especially true for younger black women writers like me who were in absolute awe of her. One day a word will be invented that encompasses all that astounding wisdom, that regal bearing, the thunderous laughter. That word would have to be spoken in all the six languages she'd mastered. But that word has not yet been birthed. What we do have are the words she left behind. And boy, did we cling to them. Boy, did I cling to them!

After I moved from Haiti to the United States at age 12, the first book I read in English was *I Know Why the Caged Bird Sings*. So enthralled was I with this extraordinarily intimate telling of her childhood that I read the book several times over an entire summer, with a dictionary. I devoured, then treasured, every word, as if they had been written just for me.

So many of us had our first encounters with Dr. Angelou's work when we needed it most. We returned to her over and over again in search of a language for our pain, as well as a clear and precise vision of who we were and could be. We also sought her out when we desperately needed a supporter, a cheerleader, someone who thought we were phenomenal.

A few years after my first novel was published—a novel based on sexual repression and abuse, which I never would have had the courage to write had I not read Dr. Angelou—I found myself sitting on a panel with her. Right before we began, I told her how reading *I Know Why the Caged Bird Sings* had saved my life. She leaned over and took my hand and in that booming, melodious voice, almost sang the words, "Well, isn't that miraculous?"

"It is miraculous," I said. Then we both had a therapeutic laugh about it.

Dr. Angelou was also miraculous. She was miraculously gifted, miraculously generous, and miraculously ubiquitous and global.

Now when my daughters and nieces and young relatives in many parts of the world write their school reports about her, or recite her poems at their graduations, I sit there and think, Isn't it miraculous that she's become such a powerful presence in my life? That she has become an indispensable gift to all of us?

She dared so many of us caged birds to sing. She told us we were the truest and most unique wonders of this world. She taught us that though our wounds might be deep, and though we might be covered with scars, we can still carry on.

For all of us who have fallen and risen again, for all of us who "have grimaced and twisted" through both heartbreak and joy, she was our Queen of Sheba, our Sojourner Truth, our Harriet Tubman, our Mary McLeod Bethune. But most important, she was uniquely our Maya Angelou.

Our Maya.

Angelou takes the stage on February 8, 2004, at Boston's Symphony Hall.

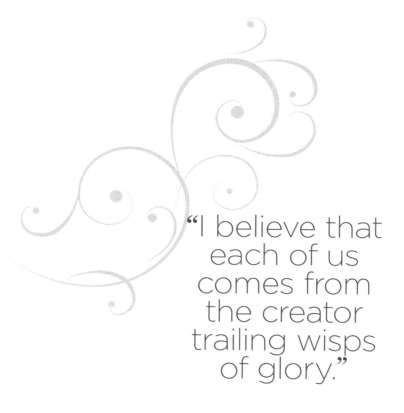

"I believe that each of us comes from the creator trailing wisps of glory."

Remembering Maya
by Pearl Cleage

Like many African-American women writers of my generation, I learned how to do my job from Maya Angelou. No, she didn't teach me how to write. She did something much harder to define. She showed me how to be a writer. She showed me how to be deeply rooted in, and unapologetically reflective of, the African-American community that had nurtured and sustained me and from that unshakable foundation, how to embrace the whole, messy, miraculous human family to which we all belong by birth and by faith.

Maya showed me how to marry my activism to my art and nurture that passionate union as a way that strengthens both. She showed me how to make the most profound truths accessible to busy, distracted, hardworking people and to share and honor their pleasure at the power of a poem to change your life when you expect it least and need it most. Her belief in the transformative power of language was the bedrock upon which Maya constructed her life's wholeness and the gift she shared with those of us fortunate enough to call her friend.

She invited me into that tight circle the first time I encountered her in the kitchen of renowned black scholar and cultural critic, Dr. Richard A. Long. As a young writer, still finding my way and my voice, I was awed and more than a little intimidated at the chance to meet the woman whose book *I Know Why the Caged Bird Sings* had shown us what real truth telling can and must be. That book gave me a bone-deep understanding of how serious I had to take this writing journey if I was going to be worthy of those who had walked it long before I came onto the scene.

I was sort of hovering around the edges of the gathering when Dr. Long took me by the hand and led me into the kitchen to meet the guest of honor who had sent him to fetch me. Maya looked up from where she was stirring a steaming pot of something that smelled delicious and smiled like she had been waiting just for me.

"Well," she said, coming around to hug me, "there you are. How is your work going?"

To my amazement, I was able to give her a coherent answer and within a minute or two, found myself engaged in conversation with Maya Angelou—Maya Angelou!—about writing!

More than most of the writers I know, Maya was comfortable talking about her process and yours. She loved the work of writing as much as she loved the finished product. But that hard work always seemed effortless. She was a person who could make words sing on the printed page without benefit of one note of music. Maya's poems especially are deceptive in their directness and simplicity. In this, she reminds me of Langston Hughes. Her poems are like a conversation conducted on a front stoop or a porch swing. They have the quiet intensity of late-night true confessions and the glorious whoop of Sunday celebration. From the first word, she draws us, her readers, into a story and style we have never known but then surrounds us and grounds us in those blood memories again, the ones that connect us in spite of ourselves. But Maya was not just a great writer. She was an amazing woman and a great friend/mentor/guide/comrade. She was funny with a laugh that made you finally understand that laughing to keep from crying is always a good strategy, no matter how serious the situation you are facing.

And now she has left us. Maya has transitioned peacefully with the grace that was always hers in life. And in this moment, we are moved to celebrate her life, not mourn her passing. We are moved to remember her truth and her passion and her laughter and her incandescent writing. We are moved to remember and to rededicate ourselves to living our lives fully, filled with joy and truth and sex and work and food and friendship and love/love/love/love.

Maya showed us who she was, and we had the good sense to believe her the first time. And every time. She is dancing with the angels...

"We may act sophisticated and worldly, but I believe we feel safest when we go inside our-selves and find home, a place where we belong and maybe the only place we really do."

Angelou brings a "Calypso Heat Wave" during a publicity photo shoot in 1957.

"Our spirituality is fed by our sensuality—

A dancing
Angelou poses
for a portrait,
circa 1950.

meaning that we are present in the world."

Angelou in a rare
performance at the
ESSENCE Music
Festival on July 4, 1997,
in New Orleans.

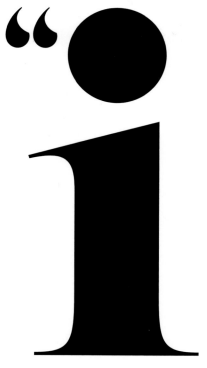

"i

alone
am
responsible
to my
God
for my
spirit."

A Maya Angelou Life Mosaic Collection by Hallmark display on January 29, 2002, in New York City. (Inset) Angelou admires a blowup of a Ghanian postage stamp in her honor on November 13, 1997.

"It costs everything to win and nothing to lose. In my mind, you might as well at least just try and give it your all."

(Clockwise, from top) Angelou, Winona Ryder and Ellen Burstyn in a scene from the film, *How to Make an American Quilt*, in 1995; Angelou and director, John Singleton, in 1993 during the filming of Singleton's film, *Poetic Justice*. Angelou wrote the poetry used in the film; Angelou shifts gears into the director's chair for the film, *Down in the Delta*, with cinematographer, William Wages (front right), on the set in 1998; Cicely Tyson and Angelou on the set of *Madea's Family Reunion* in 2006.

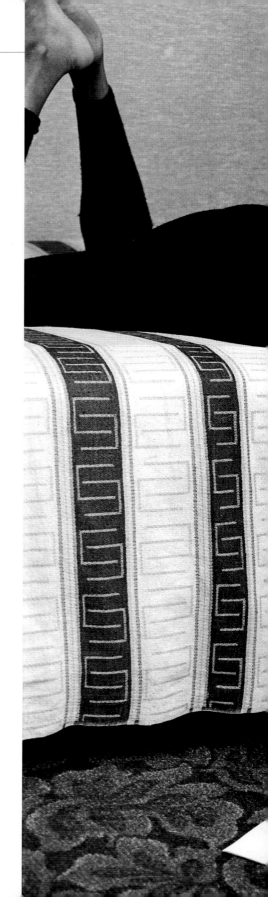

"*Give
yourself
time just
to be with
yourself.*"

Angelou greets delegates at the Democratic National Convention on July 27, 2004, in Boston.

"You use power according to how you acknowledge it inside yourself. Determine your goal or destination — and know why you want to go there."

Angelou is a proud honoree at the 24th Annual Great Sports Legends Dinner on October 6, 2009, in New York City.

Dorothy Height and Angelou attend the 25th Anniversary of the Joint Center for Political and Economic Studies in 1995.

Former President Bill Clinton congratulates Angelou after presenting her with the National Medal of Arts, December 20, 2000, in Washington, D.C.

"You can only become truly
accomplished at something you love.
Don't make money your goal.

Instead, pursue
the things
you love doing,

and then do them so well that people
can't take their eyes off you."

Malcolm X and Angelou during a trip to Ghana.

"The power I have first comes directly from being a descendant of people whose powerful history makes me humble. I would think, if I had been born anything other than Black and other than a Black American woman, that I had done something wrong in a former life and God was making me pay for it."

Angelou and then presidential candidate Senator Hillary Clinton at Wake Forest University on April 18, 2008, in Winston-Salem, North Carolina.

The Source

by asha bandele

To tell you the story of why I loved Maya Angelou is to also tell you the story of why I didn't love myself, at least not in a full way and not back then during the mean New York City teenaged years of my life. It was a post–civil rights, pro-cowboy Ronald Reagan time and my sister and I were coming of age in the prep school world of Manhattan. And as much as our parents loved and sacrificed for us, ultimately, for me, they were not shield enough against an education that whited out any and all history of who we were, ignored every brown girl song that might have been sung. We were called names sometimes, but that didn't really define our experience. Mostly what defined our experience was that we were rendered invisible.

It's quite a thing to be alive and not have it noticed, to be a human and not have it acknowledged, to have a voice and not have it be heard. It can make you almost feel insane, and then it can just break you. That's what it did to me, anyway. I had poems in my head, in my heart, but was afraid of them, afraid of my own voice. I was embarrassed about my words because nothing I had been taught or given to read seemed remotely related to the authors I was told to study if I wanted to be educated, if I wanted to matter. I wanted to matter—everyone wants to matter!—but because I couldn't find a way to do it in a world of mirrors that didn't reflect back the Black girl who was me, I concluded I didn't matter. It was with that sense that I went through high school and on into college, there but not there.

In college it wasn't a class or a professor that instigated a shift in my thinking. It was a rainy day. I was a second semester freshman, a transfer student and 16 then. I was almost always alone. Younger than my classmates, less mature and unbearably sad, I spent most days doing my work and working my training: to be unseen. And so it was that I was by myself in the campus library when the shift went down. With no real work to complete, I'd gone into the library to simply pass the time between classes and avoid the rain, and I literally stumbled on the section reserved for Black authors. I'd never seen anything so labeled. Black authors? I took a breath. I went in. Three decades on, I feel like part of me never came out of those stacks and never left the authors I found there. Mostly I picked up books of poetry, but then also one novel, *I Know Why the Caged Bird Sings*. Was this a book written just for me?

I loved every word of it, starting with the dedication Dr. Maya, as I would come to call her, wrote for her son:

AND ALL THE STRONG BLACK BIRDS OF PROMISE
who defy the odds and gods
and sing their songs

Even today as I write these words a lifetime later, my eyes swell with tears. How did she see me when all those teachers and students did not? Was I a Black Bird, and more tentatively I wondered: Did I have promise? It would be years later before I felt I could lurch toward an answer to those questions, years of shaking off that cloak of invisibility. And while there is still more work to do, I know now what I didn't know then, that like my mother before me, and my daughter after me, I am a river flowing with possibility and life. And I know that every river has a source. Dr. Maya Angelou was the source.

Angelou delivers a riveting speech at the University of Texas at Austin.

Angelou speaks during a memorial service for Betty Shabazz at Riverside Church, June 29, 1997, in Harlem.

"One isn't necessarily born with courage, but one is born with potential. Without courage, we cannot practice any other virtue with consistency. We can't be kind, true, merciful, generous or honest."

Angelou reciting her poem "On the Pulse of Morning" at the inauguration of President Bill Clinton on January 20, 1993, in Washington, D.C.

"The one hand
trying to wash itself is
a pitiful spectacle, but when
one hand washes the other,
power is increased, and
it becomes a force
to be reckoned with."

Angelou and Gloria Steinem on their way to the March on Washington's 20th anniversary, August 27, 1983.

Angelou with Andrew Young during her 80th birthday celebration on May 4, 2008, in Atlanta.

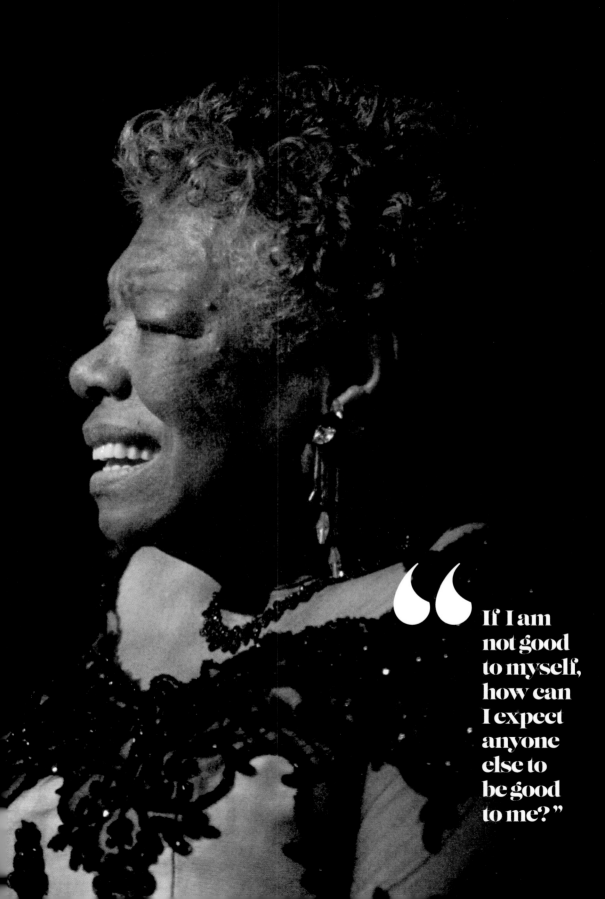

" If I am
not good
to myself,
how can
I expect
anyone
else to
be good
to me?"

59

Archbishop Desmond Tutu hugs Angelou during an awards ceremony honoring Tutu on November 21, 2008, in Washington, D.C.

It is so amazing to see where we have come from: In this country, we were meant to be hewers of wood and drawers of water, world without end. Our people not only survived that, but within 20 years of being freed from the shackles of slavery, there were Black men who were vying for the highest positions in their states as attorneys general, governors, senators. This heritage is what gives me my initial power."

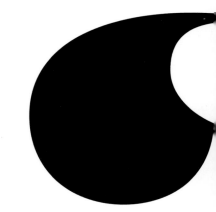

"Black women have resilience, whether we like it or not."

President Barack Obama kisses Angelou after giving her the 2010 Medal of Freedom at the White House on February 15, 2011.

"You
use
power
according
to
how
you
acknowledge
it
inside
yourself.
Determine
your
goal
or
destination
and
know
why
you
want to
go there."

Angelou takes a moment for herself at home in Winston-Salem, North Carolina, in 1986.

For Sister Maya

by Sonia Sanchez

How to speak to you of Sister Maya Angelou? How to write words so you breathe her beauty, taste her spirit, hear her intellect and genius, understand the influence she has on generations of women, men and children?

How to speak of Sister Maya Angelou, of this woman who makes "beauty in every corner of our house," of this woman heavy with the smell of clouds?

I guess I'll begin with her words: "We are a tongued folk, a race of singers and writers. Our lips shape words and rhythms which elevate our spirits and quicken our blood...I have spent over fifty years listening to my people. I write for the black voice and any ear which can hear it."

We can say anything that we want to say, but it's the prophets, the writers, the poets, the musicians, the artists who sing, who see, who soar—we love them. They come to us glittering like silver stones, their words/sounds/music so beautiful and prophetic that we catch them in mid-flight, swallow them whole. Their vision, their genius, a gift from the sea. Their lives vibrating words, songs, stories. Their ideas changing the world, shifting the earth, until it turns toward justice, peace and beauty.

We can say anything we want to say about those gatherers of beauty, rolling across the seas, earthbound though, these wearers of waves. We see them in the early morning dawn; we see them in the budding flowers. They speak a language, they play a sound that they inherited from the ancients.

I have seen how our Sister Maya crossed cities and countries to document our bones. How she stood tall as lightning, heard the trumpeters of death called Racism. Segregation. Colonialism. Greed. Sexism. Homophobia. Ignorance. And her hands caught fire as she moved us away from graveyards to our own breaths. We remember the precision of her tongue sewing itself into the sleeves of herstory and history and change.

Her poetry/prose is a festival of beauties and bones, of eyelashes and guts, of clouds and kneecaps, a transformed boulevard of peace and love where faces morphed into an ocean of butterflies. We hear the sound of rhythm on her teeth. The sound of music on her breath as her writings exploded from her eyes embroidered with pyramids.

How to tell you about a woman carrying the signature of women in her veins? I say listen...to the great blues singer Brother Montgomery: who said we all come here naked and must make arrangements for someone else while you're here, not just do for self. And that's what our dear Sister Maya did. She made arrangements for this prayer called you and me. Me and you...

How to tell you about a woman whose words gave our eyes memory? I say listen. Listen to her words......summer-bent rain moving......inside rainbows......

I say Listen. Listen. Listen.
Her words
Carry the spirit
Of creation.

"
I have
tried many
things,
failed at
many and
succeeded
at many.
"

W.F.M.

Angelou weeps
while reciting
a poem at
the Million Man
March on
October 16, 1995,
in Washington, D.C.

"To those who would try to diminish me, I say you cannot

cripple my spirit. You cannot do that. It is not yours to cripple."

71

The Book of Maya

by Melissa Harris-Perry

The Lord's Prayer, Psalm 127, John 3:16—these are verses those of us in Christian traditions know by heart. When the pastor issues the call, we know how to respond. Rooted in belief and cemented by repetition—the words are familiar catechism easily called to the surface by the right prompt.

As I sat near the rear of Wait Chapel on the campus of Wake Forest University during memorial services for Dr. Maya Angelou, I realized biblical texts are not the only one I'd learned in this way. As former President Bill Clinton began, "Every day we should 'look up and out into your sister's eyes,' " I began to whisper, "And into your brother's face." I know the words. They are from Angelou's inaugural poem, "On the Pulse of Morning." I was a junior in college and her student assistant when she penned that poem. I remember watching her read it and feeling the ground shift a bit beneath me as I realized I was witnessing history.

Oprah Winfrey stood before the mourners in Wait Chapel, visibly shaken with grief, and shared Dr. Angelou's words, "We are more alike than we are unalike." I knew to follow with, "I am a human being, nothing human is alien to me." The commonality of our humanity was a central tenet of Dr. Angelou's philosophy, and you could scarcely spend an afternoon with her without hearing it. I'd spent years in her classrooms and in her offices and at her Thanksgiving table. She taught me, through insistent repetition, that anything a human being is capable of, is something of which I too am capable. Both the monstrous horror of humanity and its epic greatness are available to me.

Throughout the memorial service friends, relatives, colleagues and dignitaries quoted from her oft-repeated wisdom. Words are things—they can manifest great harm or great good and must be deployed carefully.

Courage is the most important virtue because without it none of the other virtues can be practiced with consistency. Even in the midst of our harshest storms, the proper response is gratitude.

When I first met Dr. Angelou I was 17. My classmates and I could work ourselves into gales of laughter by admonishing one another as though we were her in utterly ridiculous circumstances. If we were rooting for the opposing basketball player to miss his foul shot, you could perform your best Angelou, "Don't speak so harshly about the other team. They are human and nothing human can be alien to us!" Although we knew she was the embodiment of greatness, we also tired of hearing the lessons repeated so often.

It wasn't until her memorial service that I fully appreciated what Dr. Angelou had done. This poet had written another book—the *Book of Maya*. Unlike the other volumes of her written, the *Book of Maya* isn't published in hard cover, it is published in us—her students. She taught us these lessons so frequently, so consistently, that they had merged with ourselves and become our truths, fully available to us, even now that she is gone.

It is important to know that the *Book of Maya* is more than the lovely sayings she contributed to Hallmark cards. The *Book of Maya* was often hard to read because Dr. Angelou's wisdom was hard won from surviving and suffering. Imbued in every line of the text she wrote in us, her students, is the insistence that all comparisons are odious and therefore all competition is fruitless. She didn't spout platitudes, she required self-examination. She refused to let us leave her presence until we engaged in serious self-reflection and critique, she made space for us to remove masks of shame, to embrace the whole messiness of our imperfection, and to sit with the discomfort of knowing that we would often fall short.

Each of her students is a chapter in the *Book of Maya*, and we will now be the authors of her legacy.

Angelou joins fellow protesters on August 28, 1963, during a demonstration at the U.S. Embassy in Accra, Ghana.

"Give

only with the intent of giving. This is pure power."

First Lady Michelle
Obama embraces
Angelou during a BET
Honors appearance on
January 14, 2012,
in Washington, D.C.

A Woman of Substance

by Maya Angelou

When I was asked during the campaign to introduce then Senator Obama and Mrs. Obama, I called Oprah Winfrey. I knew she had socialized with them. I asked her, "What is Mrs. Obama like? What should I expect?"

Oprah said simply and without hesitation, "She's the real deal." I am just so proud and so pleased to see her as our First Lady. She shows things to the world that are natural to African-American women. By that I mean her "home-iness"—her concern about growing foods for her family's kitchen and feeding them from the soil. Homegrown food is what southern Black women have always been about.

She is taking us back to our roots.

She has also—with President Obama—reintroduced the idea of romance into the American culture. Certainly past presidents have been married. And President John F. Kennedy and his wife, Jacqueline, were a beautiful couple. But when I saw the President and the First Lady dance after the inauguration—to Etta James's "At Last" of all songs—I literally wept.

It was so touching, so poignant. Lots of people had been under the impression that White people made love and Black people had sex. The way the President held her and led her. And the way she followed him...It brought me to tears.

Mrs. Obama has such an effortless grace. The clothes she wears and the way she wears them—so very beautifully—make us all feel good about ourselves as women. So much of what she wears is easily attainable and affordable to the secretaries, the teachers and all regular working women that when we see the way she is outfitted, she makes us all feel equal to her. And we feel that she is very much like us.

It's in those moments that we begin to see the fullness of her as a woman. She looks after her family—her children, her mother—just as Black women have traditionally blended generations. She loves her husband. She is intelligent. She is accessible. She is dignified but she is not aloof. She has a sense of humor but she is not a gadabout.

Michelle Obama represents all women.

—AS TOLD TO YLONDA GAULT CAVINESS

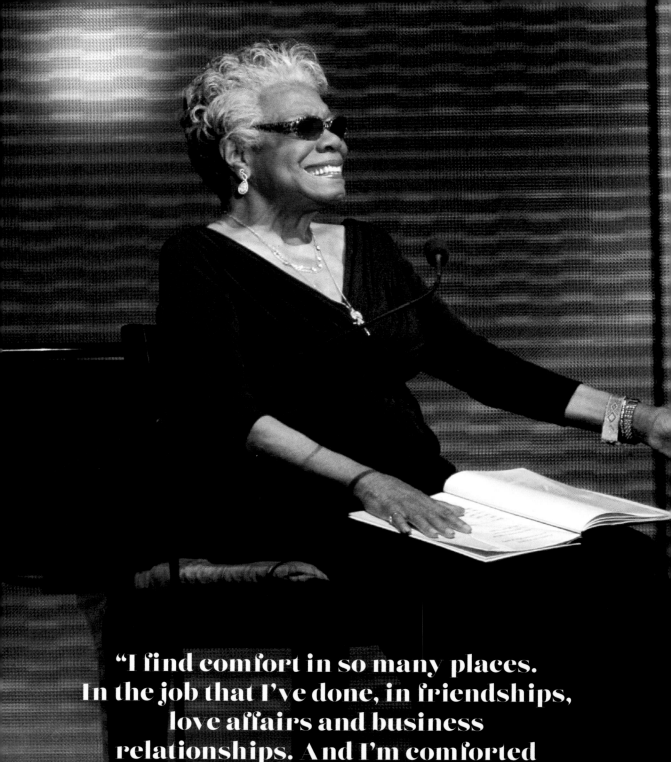

"I find comfort in so many places.
In the job that I've done, in friendships,
love affairs and business
relationships. And I'm comforted
when young people or older people say
that I've been an inspiration."

Sister
Friend

MAYA ANGELOU

"Most people don't really become friends.
They become deep and serious acquaintances.
But in a friendship you get to know the value
of another person and your values coincide.
Friends may disagree but not about serious matters.
A friend will stand for you when you are no longer able."

(Clockwise, from top) Angelou and Robin Roberts enjoy recipes that were featured in Angelou's cookbook *Great Food, All Day Long.* The interview aired on *Good Morning America,* May 5, 2011; Angelou happily cooks in the kitchen of Sugar Bar Restaurant in New York City, where she spent the day as a guest chef for a benefit dinner on September 29, 1997. Proceeds from the five-course dinner she prepared were donated to the Betty Shabazz Foundation; Angelou with English-born carpenter, Paul du Feu. The two wed in 1974 and set up house in Sonoma, California.

"My mother was the first woman who gave me my first inkling that I was a woman."

(This page, from top) Angelou shares a tender moment with her beloved mother, Vivian Baxter; Angelou with Jessica "Decca" Mitford; Angelou on December 1, 2002.

(Opposite page, from top) Angelou and son, Guy Johnson, share a laugh; Angelou and husband, Paul du Feu.

"Love recognizes no barriers. It jumps hurdles, leaps fences, penetrates walls to arrive at its destination full of hope."

"I've learned that people will forget what you said, people will forget what you did, but people will never forget how you made them feel."

Angelou enjoying a bit of quiet time outdoors, circa 1974.

Miss Maya

by Nikky Finney

April 1998, Denver, Colorado. I was reading poetry in the middle of a great stage with a warm spotlight. I had been invited to Denver by Miss Maya's great-niece Matema Hadi. The international film festival "Through My Sister's Eyes" was unfolding. Miss Maya was the main event, and I was delighted to be Miss Maya's warm-up act. I was the unknown poet reading her heart out to people who had come to see and hear the beloved queen. The audience was thick and alive with anticipation. Close to the end of my reading, I caught the shadow of someone standing stage right in the thick folds of the heavy velvet curtains. I could feel a presence, but I didn't fully turn to look. I didn't want to miss my place on the page, and I wasn't sure what I would have done had I turned and seen Maya Angelou standing there. At the end of my reading, I finally turned to look, but whoever had been there was now gone.

Miss Maya took to the stage and held court for the next two hours. Stories, poetry and song, covering the audience like a sweet snow quilt. Near the end of her time onstage, I noticed a tall Black man in a hat and suit climbing the stairs. He stopped just in front of me and called my name. "Miss Angelou would like you to join her for dinner." "Me?" and I pointed to myself. He didn't wait for my answer. He just turned to lead me down. The entire row of human beings sitting to my right erupted in applause, as if they each had been sent by my own mama to cheer me on. I was stunned at the invitation, and I smiled at them all as I followed Miss Maya's driver back down the high stairs. He led me to the open door of a very long, black limousine. The engine was running and I stepped inside. Miss Angelou was seated directly behind the driver's seat, at least 10 or 15 feet away from me. I could barely see her. The night was falling and the limousine was dark. I sat down in the first seat, squirming a little.

I didn't quite know what to do with myself in that sweet but awkward moment. Miss Angelou spoke: "Why don't I know your work, young lady?" I didn't know what to say in return. How do you answer such a question from such a person? She continued, "It was your voice that brought me out to see who you were." I had read Maya Angelou as a girl. Her voice, sotto voce, had helped bring me out into the world of writing and words. Now here was Maya Angelou telling me that my voice had brought her out of her dressing room. It was unforgettable. Voice to voice, in the tradition. Black women writers, we carry on.

"Buckle close friends to your soul."

"**Black woman to Black woman, we should be careful of anything that threatens to separate us, for if we are separated, we will be undone as a race.**"

(Opposite page, clockwise from top) Angelou and Coretta Scott King in New York City; Luther Vandross and Angelou at a *Vogue* magazine fete; Angelou receives a kiss from Harry Belafonte in Bal Harbour, Florida, January 17, 2005. (This page, clockwise from top) Ntozake Shange, Angelou and Sonia Sanchez at the Schomburg Center in Harlem, October 29, 2010; Susan L. Taylor, Dorothy Height and Angelou in Silver Spring, Maryland, December 7, 1997; Common warmly greets Angelou at her 82nd birthday party, May 20, 2010; Angelou and Johnnetta B. Cole at the Eighth Annual Black History Makers Awards Dinner in New York City, February 2, 1994; Angelou and Toni Morrison in New York City, November 20, 2013.

Black Tie and Barbecue

by Rita Dove

Like her namesake the ancient Roman earth goddess, Maya Angelou was a nurturer of both the body and the spirit. We first met around 1990 when she came to give a reading in Charlottesville, where I teach at the University of Virginia. At the reception afterward, she waved away my gushing praise, wanting instead to hear more about my maternal grandparents, on whom I had modeled characters, *Thomas and Beulah*. She had read my book and was curious: Were they still alive? Well then, how closely had I known them—and wouldn't they have been so proud?

Twenty years earlier, during my first year in college, I had devoured *I Know Why the Caged Bird Sings,* blown away by its raw biographical integrity and literary power. At about the same time I had also discovered Toni Morrison's first novel, *The Bluest Eye.* Although in some respects Morrison's world was more familiar to me, Angelou's resonated as significantly, opening my eyes to a bleakness I could not have fathomed in my rather sheltered childhood and youth.

In Black communities, we like to talk about role models, often to the point of emptying the expression of specific meaning. But I can say with certainty that, through their books, both Maya Angelou and Toni Morrison became my role models during those crucial years when a teenager sheds her self-assured exuberant naïveté and grows into a young adult plagued by insecurities and doubt. They showed me that an African-American woman could pursue her dream of becoming a writer, despite traditional white and male dominance, and that literary candor and speaking the truth to power were crucial virtues that worked in tandem with inspiration and good writing.

A few years after that first meeting, Maya rang me up out of the blue. There was no mistaking that deep, rich voice on the other end of the line. "Rita!," she said, "it is shameful. Toni received the Nobel Prize in Literature half a year ago, but she's yet to be celebrated properly. You have been poet laureate since last fall, the first Black poet laureate in the history of this country, and I have not noticed that this was properly addressed in the Black community. Something must be done. Toni and you need a party. I've decided to give you one."

And so it came that in early September 1994 Maya summoned us, and we came. Now, a party thrown by Maya Angelou exploded every definition of revelry. Guests flew into Winston-Salem, North Carolina, and were whisked by limousine to Maya's house, where a veritable Who's Who of Notable Negroes mingled under the tents erected in her backyard: Jessye Norman, Sonia Sanchez, Amiri Baraka, Oprah Winfrey, Angela Davis, ESSENCE editor Susan L. Taylor, Ashford and Simpson, to name just a few. There was a formal dress code (tuxes and gowns) for the evening's dinner and dancing: golden shawls and silken décolletés, bejeweled wrists and braids coiled into glistening labyrinths. And yet the menu was boisterously Down Home, with ribs and okra, fried chicken and biscuits. No mincing about this gig: There were hugs and guffaws, animated gesturing and licked fingers, while Maya moved through the multitudes bearing a tray of barbecued chicken, resplendent in a gilded purple caftan. She had made most of the food herself.

In the face of such magnanimous generosity, how could anybody hold back? The mood was buoyant; insecurities dissolved, petty jealousies adjourned while stories flowed, laughter arose, and we danced until the wee hours. Black tie and barbecue: It was Maya's way of showing us all how to cherish our roots while keeping our sights on the stars.

Angelou lovingly
flanked by good friends
at a 1993 reception in
her honor in
Washington, D.C.

"Have friends of both sexes. But pay special attention to your sister friends. One day lover-man may disappear, and it will be your sister friends who will be there to comfort you and tell you when it's time to get a grip."

"Black women are very intimate
with each other, and we cross cultural and social
status when talking to each other.
The housekeeper and the madam of the
house can both say,
'Ummm, ummm, ummm, umm umm,'
and everybody understands."

Angelou (in gold hat) surrounded by her circle of friends at her beloved home in Winston-Salem, North Carolina.

94

"I would have never made it without my sister friends."

Timeline

"Black wom[en]
are wielding r[eal]
actual powe[r]
and it is helpi[ng]
in concrete
measurable w[ays]
to improve t[he]
nature of ou[r]
existence."

Ange[la]
hot[o]
pro[...]
photo se[ssion]
her al[bum]
Calyps[o]

Angelou rehearsing for her now historic poetry reading of "On the Pulse of Morning."

"Through love we teach. Through love we instruct. Through love we build up."

Selected Events in the Life of a Phenomenal Woman

by Tonya Bolden

April 4, 1928

Maya Angelou is born Marguerite Annie Johnson in St. Louis, Missouri, the second child of Vivian Baxter Johnson (registered nurse) and Bailey Johnson (doorman and later armed forces dietitian). Her nickname "Maya" derives from her brother's penchant for calling her "Mya Sister."

1930's

1930

U.S. Federal Census reports a household living in South St. Louis headed by an independent real estate dealer, Thomas Baxter (58). Living with him are: wife Marguerite (53); daughters Vivian Johnson (18 and identified as a widow) and Leah (16); sons Cladwell (15), Thomas (14) and William (12); and grandchildren Bailey (3) and Marguerite (2) Johnson.

1931

Following their parents' permanent separation, Angelou and her brother are sent to Stamps, in southwest Arkansas. They are raised by their paternal grandmother, Annie Henderson, whom they call "Momma." Maya is 3; Bailey, Jr., is 4. It is two years after the great Stock Market Crash.

1934

Maternal grandfather, Thomas Baxter, dies in St. Louis at 64.

1936

While Maya and Bailey are back in St. Louis living with their mother, she, at age 8, is molested, then raped by her mother's boyfriend. Not long after he's found guilty, he is beaten to death. Following the murder young Maya becomes mute for the next five years, speaking only to her brother. The children return to Stamps.

1940's

1940

U.S. Federal Census reports a family in Stamps headed by Willie Johnson (40), manager of a grocery store. Living with him are: mother Annie (60 and a widow), a clerk in a grocery store; brother Bailey (42), a taxi driver; nephew Bailey, Jr., (13); and niece "Marguerett" (12). In Stamps Maya is befriended by Bertha Flowers, who introduces her to the world of literature. Maya graduates from Lafayette County Training School's 8th grade with honors.

1941-1942

She and her brother go West to live with their mother in the San Francisco Bay Area. Maya attends George Washington High School and earns a scholarship to study dance and drama at California Labor School. At 16, she lands a job as a streetcar conductor—a first for a Black female in San Francisco.

"What does it matter if a woman wants to frizz her hair or straighten it, or wear it natural or braid it, cut it all off or wear a wig? We can choose anything we think enhances our beauty."

1945

After graduating from high school, Maya gives birth to a son, Clyde "Guy" Johnson. During the rest of the decade, she supports herself and Guy by working an array of jobs, including waitress and cook.

1947

Maternal grandmother, Marguerite Saving Baxter, born about 1877, the year Reconstruction was abandoned, dies at 70. Marries Anastasios Angelopulos, also known as Tosh Angelos, often referred to as a sailor of Greek descent. With him, she works as a dancer and singer at popular San Francisco nightclub, Purple Onion. Here she first uses the surname that is a spin-off on her husband's: Angelou. The name lasts, but the marriage does not.

1950's

1954–1955

Angelou plays Ruby in a State Department–sponsored production of George Gershwin's opera, *Porgy and Bess*, on an international tour when the *Brown v. Board of Education* decision is handed down.

1957

Calypso Heat Wave released, in which Angelou makes her film debut, playing herself—"Miss Calypso." Cast members include Alan Arkin and Joel Grey. The producer is Sam Katzman of *Rock Around the Clock* fame. Also in 1957: Angelou's *Miss Calypso* is released. She composed five of the album's 14 songs.

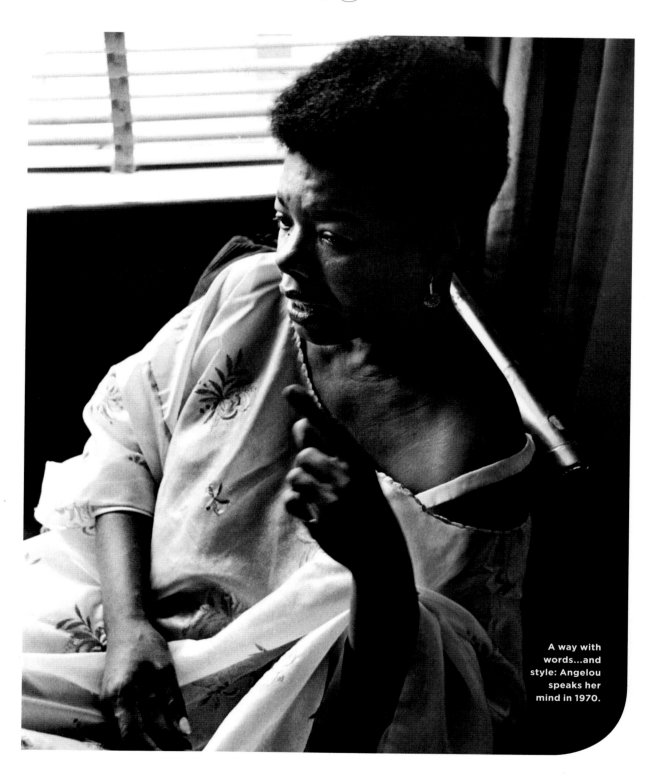

A way with words...and style: Angelou speaks her mind in 1970.

1958

"You're going to be famous," Billie Holiday told Maya Angelou in 1958, "but it won't be for singing."

The first part of the prophecy, of course, was fulfilled. The second part, in the most superficial sense, was true as well. Angelou's notoriety did not grow from the nightclub singing that she was doing to support herself and her son. Yet in another sense, Holiday was wrong. Since she first put pen to paper, Maya Angelou has been singing. Also in 1958: Maya moves to New York City and joins the legendary Harlem Writers Guild, founded in 1950 by historian Dr. John Henrik Clarke, author Rosa Guy, author John Oliver Killens and other writer/scholar-activists. *Cabaret for Freedom* is co-written and produced with Godfrey Cambridge at New York City's Village Gate theater. This variety show is a fund-raiser for the Southern Christian Leadership Conference (SCLC). Two years later, Martin Luther King, Jr., asks Angelou to serve as the SCLC Northern Coordinator.

"There's no such thing as regression in life, only constant change."

An animated Angelou being interviewed at one of her homes on April 8, 1978.

103

1960's

1960

Opening night of Jean Genet's *The Blacks* at New York City's St. Mark's Playhouse. Angelou was cast as the Queen, along with fellow actors James Earl Jones, Louis Gossett, Jr., Cicely Tyson and Godfrey Cambridge.

Romantically linked to South African freedom fighter, Vusumzi Make. Roughly six months after accepting the position, Angelou resigns from her SCLC post. Angelou moves to Cairo with her son. There she works as an editor of *Arab Observer*, an English-language weekly.

1961–1963

After her relationship with Make ends, Maya relocates (with her son) to Ghana where she teaches at the University of Ghana's School of Music and Drama, serves as an editor of *The African Review* and writes for the *Ghanaian Times*. She also enjoys the company of other expats, among them W.E.B. Du Bois, who dies in Ghana on August 27, 1963, the eve of the March on Washington for Jobs and Freedom.

1964

Returns to America with plans to work on the strengthening of the Organization of Afro-American Unity, spearheaded by Malcolm X, who was assassinated on February 21, 1965.

1966

Premiere of Jean Anouilh's *Medea* at Theater of Being in Hollywood. Angelou plays "Nurse". Also in 1966: Lecturer at California State University, Sacramento.

April 4, 1968

Maya turns 40 the day Martin Luther King, Jr., is assassinated. Also in 1968: For National Educational Television, Angelou writes a series of ten one-hour programs on African culture in America: *Black, Blues, Black*.

1968

Father Bailey James Johnson dies in San Diego at 66.

1970's

1970

I Know Why the Caged Bird Sings published, a memoir of the agonies and ecstasies as she matures into adulthood during the Depression and World War II. An international best seller, it is nominated for a National Book Award and is the first installment in what will be a seven-volume memoir. Also in 1970: Writer in Residency at University of Kansas and Chubb Fellowship Award from Yale University.

1971

"Just Give Me a Cool Drink of Water 'Fore I Diiie" (poetry) published, then nominated for a Pulitzer Prize.

Angelou takes the stage in New York City during a 1976 TV taping of the *Ladies' Home Journal* Woman of the Year presentation, with then First Lady Betty Ford (third from right).

1972

Georgia, Georgia released; screenplay and score by Angelou, directed by Swedish writer Stig Björkman. The film is nominated for a Pulitzer Prize and also marks the first screenplay by a Black woman in America.

1973

Premiere of Jerome Kilty's *Look Away* at the New York City's Playhouse Theater. Maya is nominated for a Tony Award for her portrayal in this post–Civil War, two-women play of Elizabeth Keckley,

Female Eunuch. Of Angelou and du Feu, *People* magazine says that "to their neighbors in Northern California" the newlyweds "are beauty and the bloke." She is 45; he is 38. Also in 1974: *Gather Together in My Name* (memoir about her life as a young single mother) published, and she's awarded Distinguished Visiting Professorship at Wake Forest University in Winston-Salem, North Carolina, Wichita State University and California State University, Sacramento. Angelou also wrote and directed the screenplay, *All Day Long*.

"Any idea is at its best when it liberates."

Mary Todd Lincoln's dressmaker. Geraldine Page plays the former First Lady. Also in 1973: She receives an honorary degree from Portland State University. Maya becomes the recipient of more than 50 honorary degrees in her lifetime.

1974

Weds Paul du Feu, a Welsh master carpenter formerly married to Germaine Greer, author of the groundbreaking *The*

1975

"Oh Pray My Wings Are Gonna Fit Me Well" (poetry) published. Also in 1975: Maya becomes a Rockefeller Foundation Scholar in Italy, Scholar-in-Residence at the Bellagio Study & Conference Center and appointed member of American Revolution Bicentennial Council by President Gerald R. Ford. She was fluent in six languages including Arabic, Italian, and West African Fanti.

1976

Singin' and Swingin' and Gettin' Merry Like Christmas (memoir of her early twenties) published. Also in 1976: Named Woman of the Year in Communication by *Ladies' Home Journal.* Her one-act musical *And Still I Rise* debuts at the Ensemble Theater in Oakland.

1977

TV miniseries based on Alex Haley's novel *Roots: The Saga of an American Family* airs. Angelou plays Yaisa/Nyo Boto, earning an Emmy nomination.

1978

And *Still I Rise* (poetry) published.

1979

Her teleplay based on *Caged Bird* is broadcast with Diahann Carroll, Ruby Dee and Madge Sinclair. Constance Good plays young Maya.

1980's

1981

Maya is appointed Reynolds Professor of American Studies chair at Wake Forest University. She teaches a variety of courses, including "African Culture and Impact on U.S." and "Shakespeare and the Human Condition." Also in 1981, *The Heart of a Woman* (memoir about her New York–Cairo days) published.

1983

Shaker, Why Don't You Sing? (poetry) published.

1986

All God's Children Need Traveling Shoes (memoir about her days in Ghana) published.

1987

Now Sheba Sings the Song (poetry) published, illustrated by Caldecott Honor winner and friend, Tom Feelings.

1990's

1990

Receives Candace Award from National Coalition of 100 Black Women. Also in 1990: *I Shall Not Be Moved* (poetry) published.

1991

Mother Vivian Althea Baxter dies in Winston-Salem at 79.

1992

ESSENCE Woman of the Year Award winner.

January 20, 1993

Angelou recites "On the Pulse of Morning" at President Bill Clinton's inauguration, who grew up in Hope, Arkansas, about 30 miles from Stamps. This is the first time a

(Left) Selected works of Dr. Maya Angelou including her groundbreaking 1970 debut, *I Know Why the Caged Bird Sings* and her Grammy award-winning "Phenomenal Woman: Four Poems Celebrating Women."

"Nothing is owed me, and I take nothing for granted—not my life, not my gifts, not my talents, not love."

"I direct my energy toward moving on, moving ahead."

Angelou at the 1985 commencement at Wake Forest University in Winston-Salem, North Carolina.

poet made a presentation at a presidential inauguration since Robert Frost recited "The Gift Outright" at JFK's in 1961. In the wake of "Pulse," *Caged Bird* becomes a best seller once again. Also in 1993: "Life Doesn't Frighten Me" (poem) published with paintings by Jean-Michel Basquiat, as well as "On the Pulse of Morning" and "Wouldn't Take Nothing for My Journey Now" (wisdom talk).

1994

Maya wins a Grammy for Best Spoken Word or Non-Musical Album for *On the Pulse of Morning*. Also in 1994: NAACP's Spingarn Medal.

1995

"Phenomenal Woman: Four Poems Celebrating Women" published, her recording of which will receive a Grammy for Best Spoken Word or Non-Musical Album.

1995

At the Million Man March that took place in Washington, D.C., Angelou recites poem "From a Black Woman to a Black Man."

1998

Down in the Delta released, directed by Angelou. Cast includes Al Freeman, Jr., Esther Rolle, Wesley Snipes and Alfre Woodard.

Also in 1998: Inducted into the National Women's Hall of Fame.

1999

Brother Bailey Johnson, Jr., dies in Winston-Salem at 72.

2000's

2000

Awarded the National Medal of Arts from President Bill Clinton in Washington, D.C.

2002

A Song Flung Up to Heaven (memoir on her return to America from Africa) published. Her recording will eventually win a Grammy for Best Spoken Word Album.

2004

Hallelujah! The Welcome Table: A Lifetime of Memories with Recipes (cookbook) published.

2005

"Amazing Peace: A Christmas Poem" published, read at the 2005 White House tree-lighting ceremony.

2006

"Mother: A Cradle to Hold Me" (poetry) published.

2008

Letter to My Daughter (essays) published. Also in 2008: Recipient of the Ford Theater's Lincoln Medal.

2010's

2010

New York Public Library announces that its Schomburg Center for Research in Black Culture has acquired "The Maya Angelou Collection of Personal Papers and Materials Documenting 40 Years of the Writer's Literary Career and Phenomenal Rise to World Acclaim." This collection includes published and unpublished writings, as well as correspondence with James Baldwin, Rosa Guy, Abbey Lincoln, Malcolm X and

"As a Black
woman, I know
where I have
come from."

Gordon Parks. Also in 2010: *Great Food, All Day Long: Cook Splendidly, Eat Smart* (cookbook) published.

2011

Receives Presidential Medal of Freedom from President Barack Obama, the highest civilian award.

Category: Literature. Obama praises Angelou for rising above an abusive childhood to inspire others. Her voice, he says, has "spoken to millions, including my mother, which is why my sister is named Maya."

A hugely admired professor, Dr. Angelou teaches for the last time at Wake Forest in 2011. (She had plans to return to teaching at Wake Forest in the Fall of 2014).

2013

Mom & Me & Mom (memoir) published. Also in 2013: Receives National Book Foundation's Literarian Award for Outstanding Service to the American Literary Community, receives Mailer Prize for Lifetime Achievement from the Norman Mailer Center, and at Wake Forest University, delivers opening remarks for a celebration of the campus-wide "Dignity and Respect Campaign."

May 21, 2014

When *Kansas City Star* reporter Edward M. Eveld asks her about the topic of her scheduled talk on June 10 at the Kaufman Center for the Performing Arts, Angelou replies "Courage and love and laughter and the moon and cooking." She adds, "I think courage is the most important of all the virtues. Without courage you can't practice any other virtue consistently."

May 28, 2014

Dr. Maya Angelou dies in her home in Winston-Salem around eight o'clock in the morning.

May 30, 2014–June 30, 2014

"Phenomenal Woman: Maya Angelou 1928–2014," an exhibit at the Schomburg Center for Research in Black Culture, in Harlem.

Maya Angelou

Her Phenomenal Life & Poetic Journey

Credits